HEART ON A PLATE

HEART ON A ♥ PLATE

Emma Marsden

◨ SQUARE PEG

Published by Square Peg 2014

10 9 8 7 6 5 4 3 2 1

Copyright © Square Peg 2014

First published in Great Britain in 2013 by
Square Peg
Random House, 20 Vauxhall Bridge Road,
London SW1V 2SA
www.vintage-books.co.uk

Addresses for companies within The Random House Group
Limited can be found at:
www.randomhouse.co.uk/offices.htm
The Random House Group Limited Reg. No. 954009

A CIP catalogue record for this book is available from the
British Library

ISBN 978 0 22 409868 7

The Random House Group Limited supports the Forest
Stewardship Council®(FSC®), the leading international
forest-certification organisation. Our books carrying the
FSC label are printed on FSC®-certified paper. FSC is the
only forest-certification scheme supported by the leading
environmental organisations, including Greenpeace. Our
paper procurement policy can be found at
www.randomhouse.co.uk/environment

Photography by Sarah Cuttle
Food styling by Emma Marsden and Ellie Jarvis

Typeset and designed by Anna Green
at www.siulendesign.com

Printed and bound in China by C&C Offset Printing Co., Ltd

We've included some clever ways to create hearts without requiring any specialist equipment, but there are brilliant heart-shaped utensils you can buy cheaply. It would be useful to have a set of heart-shaped pastry cutters, and a couple of recipes require heart-shaped dishes, but you can exercise your artistic skills and shape your hearts freehand if you prefer.

Unless stated otherwise:
• All eggs are medium
• All spoon measurements are level
• All vegetables should be peeled

Leabharlanna Poibli Chathair Bhaile Átha Cliath
Dublin City Public Libraries

CONTENTS ❤

10 Meringue Kisses

14 Spiced Chocolate Mousse with Shortbread Hearts

18 Big Red Velvet Heart

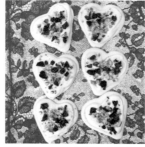

22 Fruit and Nut White Chocolate Bark

24 Heart Cookies

28 Filo Pastry Hearts

30 Marshmallow Hearts

34 Marzipan Hearts

38 Raspberry Puffs

40 Strawberry Heart Champagne Jellies

42 Chocolate and Strawberry Truffles

46 Lace Heart Pancakes

50 Heart Palmiers

54 Blackberry Hearts in Cream Jellies

58 Sopapillas

60 Lovely Lunchbox Muffin

66 Loveheart Salt and Pepper Bagels with Roasted Tomato Soup

70 Summer Love Minestrone with Pesto

72 Ricotta and Herb Ravioli

76 Rose-Lover's Salad with Boiled Egg Hearts

80 His and Hers Brekkie

82 Luxury Fish Pie

84 Braveheart Pie

88 Fish-Lover's Pasta

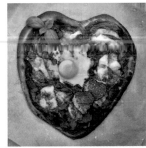

92 Heartburger in a Bun

94 Big Heart Pizza with Truffle

98 Five-spice Duck Heart Pie Pops

100 Steak Frites pour Deux

104 Champagne-Lover's Treat

108 Zesty Ice Hearts

SWEET

MERINGUE KISSES

The rich, creamy filling and tart cherries perfectly balance these sweet, light-as-a-feather meringues.

SERVES 4

3 large egg whites
about 200g caster sugar
pink food colouring
50g white chocolate, chopped

For the filling
300ml double cream
1 tbsp icing sugar, plus extra for sprinkling
about 4 tbsp cherry jam

To serve
8 fresh ripe cherries

You will need
6.5cm heart-shaped cutter
piping bag fitted with a 1cm round nozzle

Preheat the oven to 110°C/90°C fan/gas ½.

Drawing freehand or using a 6.5cm heart-shaped cutter as a template, draw 8 hearts on to 2 sheets of baking parchment. Turn the sheets over and lay them on 2 baking sheets. There's no need to grease the paper as meringue will later be used to secure the corners.

Weigh a spotlessly clean bowl, then weigh the egg whites in it. Calculate their weight, double it and weigh that quantity of caster sugar into a separate bowl.

Whisk the egg whites until they stand in soft peaks and the fluffy mixture doesn't slip around in the bowl. You should be able to turn it upside down over your head without the mixture falling out. Whisk in the sugar, a tablespoon at a time, making sure each spoonful dissolves completely before adding the next. Dip a cocktail stick into the food colouring and add it to the meringue until you reach the depth of colour you want.

Dot a little of the meringue under the corners of each piece of parchment to secure the paper to the baking sheet.

Spoon the rest of the meringue into a piping bag fitted with a 1cm round nozzle and pipe inside the traced heart templates. Bake for about 1½ hours, until the meringues come away easily from the paper. Leave to cool in the oven.

Set a heatproof bowl over a pan of simmering water, making sure the bottom of the bowl does not touch the water. Melt the white chocolate in the bowl, then spoon it over the base of each meringue and leave to set.

Whip the cream and icing sugar in a bowl until thick and glossy. Swirl in the cherry jam.

Take 2 meringue hearts and sandwich them together with the sweet jam cream. Serve dusted with a little extra icing sugar and a couple of ripe cherries.

SPICED CHOCOLATE MOUSSE WITH SHORTBREAD HEARTS

The flavours of cardamom and orange in this mousse, served with crisp spiced shortbread, complement each other beautifully. If you prefer a slightly less rich mousse, use 25g milk chocolate and 75g dark chocolate.

SERVES 4

100g dark chocolate (about 50% cocoa solids),
   broken into pieces
1 tsp brandy
10g butter
seeds from 2 cardamom pods, ground
1 orange
2 large eggs, separated
25g caster sugar
edible gold dust

For the shortbread
25g golden caster sugar, plus extra for dusting
50g butter
75g plain flour, plus extra, for dusting
a large pinch of mixed spice
a large pinch of salt

You will need
4cm heart-shaped cutter
5cm heart-shaped cutter

SPICED CHOCOLATE MOUSSE CONTINUED

Preheat the oven to 190°C/170°C fan/gas 5.

First make the shortbread. Beat the sugar and butter together in a bowl until the mixture looks soft and creamy. Stir in the flour, spice and salt to make a crumbly texture, then bring it all together with your hands to make a dough.

Lightly dust a board with flour and roll out the dough to a thickness of 3mm. Stamp out 4 hearts with a 4cm heart-shaped cutter, and another 4 hearts with a 5cm heart-shaped cutter. Transfer them all to a plate and chill in the fridge for 15 minutes.

Once chilled, use a skewer to prick small holes around each heart to create a decorative border and bake for 15–20 minutes, until just coloured. Transfer to a wire rack and dust liberally with caster sugar.

Now make the mousse. Set a heatproof bowl over a pan of simmering water, making sure the bottom of the bowl does not touch the water. Put the chocolate pieces, brandy and butter in the bowl and slowly melt together. Grate in the zest from half the orange and stir in the ground cardamom. Take the bowl off the heat and set aside to cool.

Beat together the egg yolks and sugar. Carefully stir this into the chocolate mixture.

In a separate clean bowl, beat the egg whites until they stand in soft peaks. Fold a third of the egg whites into the chocolate mixture, then fold in the remainder. Divide the mousse between 4 teacups and chill in the fridge for at least 2 hours.

Just before serving, peel 8 thin strips of the remaining zest from the orange. Arrange 2 strips in a heart shape on top of each mousse. Sprinkle over a little gold dust then serve with the biscuits.

BIG RED VELVET HEART

This moist, single-layered gateau of deep red velvety sponge is topped with a contrasting cream cheese frosting.

SERVES 12

125g butter, softened
275g golden caster sugar
3 eggs
200g plain flour
25g cocoa powder, plus extra for dusting
125ml buttermilk
½ tsp bicarbonate of soda
½ tbsp white wine vinegar
2 tbsp red food colouring paste, such as
    Sugarflair red extra

For the frosting
75g butter
150g icing sugar
300g cream cheese

You will need
square 16–17cm cake tin
round 15cm cake tin

Preheat the oven to 180°C/160°C fan/gas 4.

Butter and line a square 16–17cm cake tin and a round 15cm cake tin with greaseproof paper.

Whisk together the butter and sugar in a large bowl until soft and creamy. Gradually whisk in the eggs, adding a spoonful of plain flour if the mixture looks as if it will curdle.

Sift over the remaining flour with the cocoa powder buttermilk. Mix the bicarbonate of soda with the vinegar and fold into the mixture along with the red food colouring.

Divide the mixture between the tins, giving a spoonful extra to the square tin (as it's slightly larger). Bake for about 30 minutes, until a skewer inserted into the centre comes out clean. Turn out on to a wire rack to cool.

BIG RED VELVET HEART CONTINUED

To make the frosting, beat together the butter
and icing sugar, then fold in the cream cheese
until the mixture is smooth.

Remove the paper from the cakes. Slice the
edges off the square sponge to neaten it. Cut
the round cake in half to make 2 semicircles.
Position the square sponge in the centre of a
35cm cake plate and position the 2 semicircles
against 2 of the sides to create a heart shape.
You might need to trim a little off the top of
each semicircle so that they're the same level
as the square cake.

Spoon the cream cheese frosting all over the
top and sides of the cake, smoothing it down
with a palette knife. To decorate, position a
paper doily on top of the cake and lightly dust
some cocoa powder over the holes. Move the
doily around the cake, dusting as you go, to
create a pretty pattern.

FRUIT AND NUT
WHITE CHOCOLATE BARK

Top these heart-shaped thins with your favourite dried fruit and nut combination for a really special present.

MAKES 6

150g white chocolate, broken into pieces
10g dried cranberries
10g pecan nuts, toasted and roughly chopped
edible pink glitter

You will need
6cm heart-shaped cutter
sugar thermometer (optional)

Set a heatproof bowl over a pan of simmering water, making sure the bottom of the bowl does not touch the water. Melt the chocolate in the bowl, then take it off the heat and set aside to cool for 15 minutes. If you want to temper the chocolate (so that it crystallises evenly and retains its shine), put a thermometer into it and wait until the temperature drops to 28–29°C.

Drawing freehand or using a 6cm cutter as a template, draw 6 hearts on a piece of baking parchment. Turn the parchment over so that the outlines are on the underside and lay it on a baking sheet.

Spread a teaspoonful of chocolate inside each heart shape using the back of a spoon. Cover each base with another thin layer of chocolate. Continue layering until you have heart bases of equal thickness.

Scatter the cranberries and pecans over the hearts, then sprinkle them with pink glitter. Leave to set in a cool place for an hour or 2 before serving.

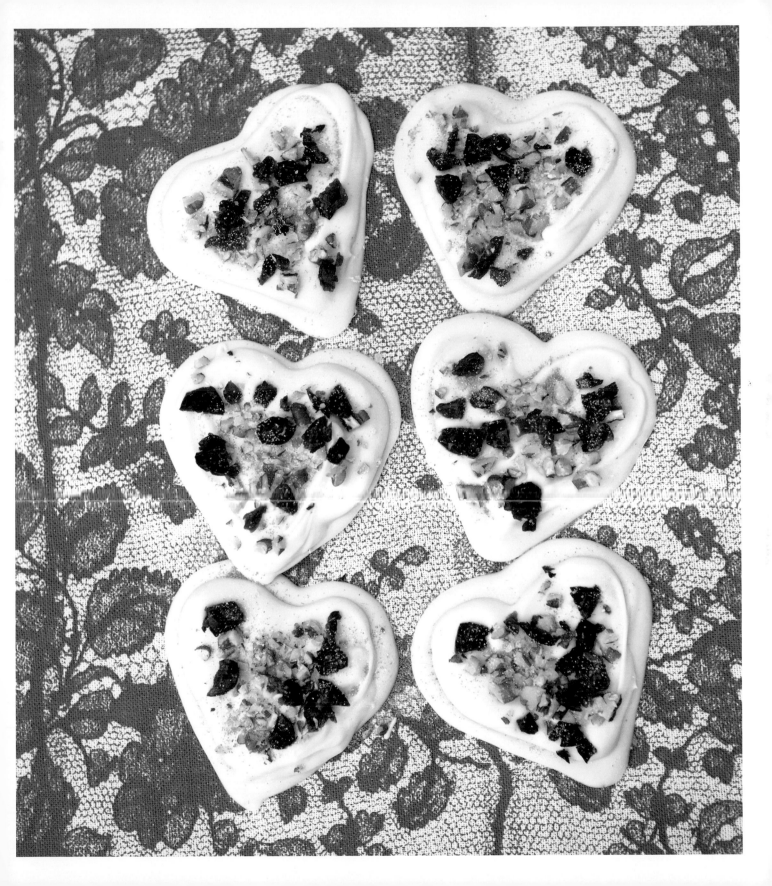

HEART COOKIES

These crisp lemon biscuits are flooded with knicker-pink icing and dotted with pretty white hearts.

MAKES 8

75g butter
75g golden caster sugar
zest of ½ lemon
1–2 tbsp lemon juice
150g plain flour, sifted, plus extra for dusting

For the icing
250g icing sugar
1 egg white
red food colouring

You will need
7cm heart-shaped cutter
piping bag fitted with a 1–2mm round
  nozzle

Preheat the oven to 190°C/170°C fan/gas 5. Line 2 baking sheets with baking parchment.

Beat the butter, sugar and lemon zest together in a bowl. Stir in the lemon juice and flour until the mixture looks crumbly, then form into a ball with your hands. Place on a lightly floured board and knead to make a smooth dough. Shape into a circle then wrap in cling film and chill in the fridge for 15 minutes.

Lightly flour a board and roll out the dough until it's about 3mm thick. Cut out 8 biscuits either freehand or using a 7cm cutter, rerolling the dough as necessary. Transfer the cookies to the prepared baking sheets and chill in the fridge for 10 minutes.

Bake for 10–12 minutes, until golden. Cool on a wire rack.

To make the icing, whisk half the icing sugar in a bowl with the egg white. Continue to add the icing sugar, a spoonful at a time, until it's all mixed in. Whisk well for 5–10 minutes, until the mixture is thick.

HEART COOKIES CONTINUED

Put a heaped tablespoon of icing into a dish and set aside. Dip a cocktail stick into the food colouring and stir it into the rest of the icing. Whisk well to incorporate the colour completely. Add more colouring until you have the desired shade.

Spoon one-third of the pink icing into a piping bag fitted with a 1–2mm round nozzle. Pipe around the edge of a biscuit to create a raised border. Spoon more of the pink icing into the middle of the biscuit and use the back of a spoon to flood inside the border.

Use a cocktail stick to place small dots of white icing around the edges, or all over, the pink icing on the biscuit, then drag a clean cocktail stick from top to bottom of each dot to create heart shapes. Allow to set while you decorate the remaining biscuits in the same way.

Store in an airtight container and enjoy within 5 days.

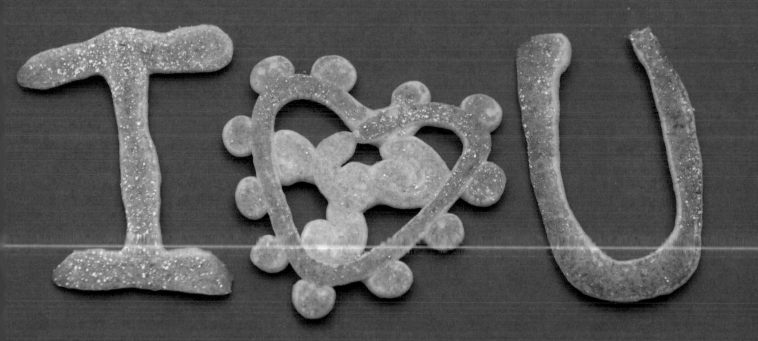

FILO PASTRY HEARTS

These bite-sized treats have a filling of hazelnuts and chocolate, all wrapped up in buttery pastry. They make a great alternative to the traditional truffles served with coffee.

MAKES 15

50g hazelnuts
10g demerara sugar
25g dark chocolate (50–70% cocoa solids),
    finely chopped
25g milk chocolate, roughly chopped
zest of ½ lemon or orange
1 tbsp cocoa powder
1 tbsp brandy
1 egg yolk
3–5 sheets filo pastry
butter, melted
icing sugar, for dusting

Toast the hazelnuts in a dry pan until golden. Set them aside to cool, then chop roughly and whiz in a blender until coarsely ground. Transfer the nuts to a bowl and stir in the sugar, dark chocolate, citrus zest, cocoa, brandy and egg yolk.

Using your fingers, shape the mixture into 15 hearts and transfer to a plate. Chill for 20 minutes.

Preheat the oven to 200°C/180°C fan/gas 6. Line a baking sheet with baking parchment.

Lay a sheet of filo pastry on a board and brush with melted butter. Cut the sheet lengthways into 4 equal strips. Carefully wrap each heart with a strip of pastry, brushing liberally with butter once the chocolate is completely covered.

Transfer the pastry hearts to the prepared baking sheet and bake for 8–10 minutes, until golden. Set aside to cool on the sheet and dust with icing sugar to serve.

MARSHMALLOW HEARTS

Pillow-soft marshmallows and rich, dark hot chocolate are a match made in heaven. This recipe makes plenty, and the marshmallows will keep in a cool place for up to a week if wrapped in cling film.

SERVES 4

120ml cold water
6 gelatine leaves
200g granulated sugar
125ml golden syrup
a good pinch of salt
1 tsp pure vanilla extract
pink food colouring
vegetable oil, for greasing
icing sugar, for dusting

To serve
400ml milk
75g dark chocolate (about 50% cocoa solids)

You will need
square 20–24cm cake tin
sugar thermometer
4cm heart-shaped cutter

Lightly oil a square 20–24cm cake tin and line it with baking parchment (the smaller the tin, the thicker the finished marshmallow). Sift a little icing sugar over the base.

Pour half the water into a bowl and add the gelatine. Set aside to soak for 15 minutes, until softened.

Pour the rest of the water into a pan and add the sugar, golden syrup and salt. Place over a low heat and warm gently to dissolve the sugar. Place a thermometer in the pan and simmer the mixture for about 10 minutes, until the temperature reaches 115°C. Take off the heat and set aside.

MARSHMALLOW HEARTS CONTINUED

Using an electric whisk, slowly whisk the gelatine while gradually pouring in the sugar syrup in a thin stream down inside the edge of the bowl. Continue to whisk, increasing the speed gradually, until the mixture is very thick and stiff. This may take up to 10 minutes.

Add the vanilla extract and a dot of food colouring on the end of a cocktail stick. Whisk again to combine.

Spoon the mixture into the prepared tin and dust well with icing sugar. Leave to set overnight at room temperature.

Turn the marshmallow out of the tin and use a 4cm cutter to stamp out hearts.

To serve, bring the milk to the boil in a pan then whisk in the chocolate until smooth. Divide between bowls or mugs. Float a marshmallow on top of each hot chocolate drink and enjoy immediately.

MARZIPAN HEARTS

If you're short of time, you can cheat in this recipe by using naturally coloured ready-made marzipan instead of home-made – you'll need about 200g.

MAKES 10–12

100g ground almonds
50g golden caster sugar
50g icing sugar, plus extra for dusting
2–3 tbsp beaten egg
1 tsp orange juice
red food colouring
edible gold glitter

You will need
4cm heart-shaped cutter
10–12 lollipop sticks

Put the ground almonds into a bowl with the sugars. Make a well in the middle and stir in the beaten egg and orange juice with a wooden spoon. Use your hands to knead everything together into a paste, then wrap in cling film and chill in the fridge for 1 hour.

Lightly dust a board with icing sugar and roll out the chilled marzipan until it's about 1cm thick. Stamp out 10–12 hearts using a 4cm cutter, rerolling the marzipan as necessary.

Push a lollipop stick through the pointed end of each heart and lay out to dry on a sheet of baking parchment for 4 hours, turning halfway through.

Once the marzipan is dry, toast both sides of each heart with a blowtorch or under a hot grill until lightly browned. Brush the top with the red food colouring, then flick gold glitter all over the surface, Jackson Pollock-style. Allow to dry, then serve.

RASPBERRY PUFFS

Here's a sweet version of the classic 1970s vol-au-vent, brought bang up to date with a mascarpone and cream filling topped with raspberries.

MAKES 8–10

500g puff pastry
100g mascarpone
200ml double cream
2 tsp icing sugar
a little milk (optional)
200g raspberries
a little butter for greasing
a little plain flour, for dusting
icing sugar, for dusting

You will need
7cm heart-shaped cutter
4cm heart-shaped cutter

Preheat the oven to 220°C/200° fan/gas 7. Lightly grease a baking sheet.

Lightly dust a work surface with flour. Roll out the puff pastry, rolling in one direction only, until it is 5mm thick. Use a 7cm cutter to stamp out 8–10 hearts, then press a 4cm cutter halfway through the centre of each one. Transfer to the prepared baking sheet and chill in the fridge for 20 minutes.

Bake the hearts for 20 minutes, then let cool for 2 minutes before carefully removing the inner hearts, keeping them whole. Set these mini hearts aside on a plate.

Scrape out any uncooked pastry dough from the larger hearts and return them to the oven for a couple of minutes to dry out. Set aside to cool.

Carefully fold the mascarpone, double cream and icing sugar together in a bowl. If the mixture is too thick to spoon in, stir in a little milk to soften it. Divide the mascarpone cream among the hearts and top with raspberries. Place the mini pastry hearts on the side and dust the finished vol-au-vents with icing sugar.

STRAWBERRY HEART CHAMPAGNE JELLIES

Here's a delicately boozy way to finish a midsummer dinner party. The jellies can be made up to 8 hours ahead. Serve with a spoonful of softly whipped double cream sweetened with icing sugar.

SERVES 4

6 gelatine leaves
450ml sparkling wine
50g golden caster sugar, plus a little extra
4 strawberries

Put the gelatine leaves in a bowl and cover in cold water. Set aside to soak for 10 minutes.

Pour the wine into a pan over a low heat and add the sugar. Heat gently to dissolve the sugar, then bring to the boil. Turn off the heat.

Lift the gelatine out of the bowl and squeeze out any excess water. Stir the gelatine into the hot wine until dissolved.

Slice the strawberries in half, then, using a small knife, carve the top of each one into a heart shape.

Set out 4 glass dishes. Spoon 2 hearts into each dish then divide the jelly mixture between them. Set aside to cool, then chill in the fridge for at least 5 hours until firm.

CHOCOLATE AND STRAWBERRY TRUFFLES

These luxurious truffles – rich, dense ganache covered with a thin shell of dark chocolate – have an intense flavour from the freeze-dried berries.

MAKES 6 GENEROUS-SIZED CHOCOLATES

250g dark chocolate (70% cocoa solids), finely chopped
1 tbsp crushed freeze-dried strawberries, plus extra for sprinkling
75ml double cream
1 tbsp strawberry liqueur

You will need
plastic tray, about the size of a margarine tub
4cm heart-shaped cutter
sugar thermometer (optional)

Line a small, shallow container, about the size of a margarine tub, with cling film. Line a baking sheet with baking parchment.

Put 75g of the chocolate and the crushed strawberries into a bowl and set it aside.

Pour the cream and strawberry liqueur into a pan and bring to the boil. Pour it immediately over the chocolate and strawberries and stir until the chocolate has melted. Spoon the mixture into the lined container and chill in the fridge for 1 hour.

Lift the chilled ganache out of the container and place it on a board. Stamp out heart shapes using a 4cm cutter and place them on a plate. Return to the fridge to chill.

Set a heatproof bowl over a pan of simmering water, making sure the bottom of the bowl does not touch the water. Add the remaining chocolate and, as soon as it has melted, remove the bowl from the pan and set aside to rest with a thermometer in it until the temperature drops to 31–32°C. (This part of the process is not essential – you can simply cool the chocolate for 10–15 minutes – but tempering ensures it remains smooth and glossy. If you don't temper the chocolates you will need to store them in the fridge.)

CHOCOLATE & STRAWBERRY TRUFFLES
CONTINUED

Remove the truffles from the fridge and quickly lower one of the hearts into the chocolate with a fork until it is completely coated, then transfer to the lined baking sheet. Sprinkle with crushed strawberries before the chocolate has set. Repeat with the remaining truffles. You will need to work quickly so that the truffles don't melt and lose their shape before they're coated. Leave to set.

Pack the truffles in a box and chill until ready to give as a present or serve.

Cook's tip
Roll any remaining ganache into small balls, then coat with crushed freeze-dried strawberries to decorate.

LACE HEART PANCAKES

These pancakes make a charming breakfast treat. All you need is a squeezy bottle and a steady hand to create the delicate lacy effect. If you can't get hold of buttermilk, use half milk and half yoghurt instead.

SERVES 4–6

150g self-raising flour
½ tsp bicarbonate of soda
a good pinch of salt
25g golden caster sugar
a good pinch of cinnamon
1 egg
175ml buttermilk
50ml milk
30g butter, melted and cooled
vegetable oil
icing sugar, for dusting

You will need:
large squeezy bottle
large-holed funnel

Sift the flour, bicarbonate of soda and salt into a bowl. Stir in the sugar and cinnamon, then make a well in the middle.

Whisk together the egg, buttermilk, milk and butter in a jug. Pour into the well in the flour mixture and stir gently to make a thick batter. Pour half the mixture into a large squeezy bottle using a large-holed funnel.

Heat a frying pan over a medium heat for a minute or 2 until hot. Add about ½ teaspoon vegetable oil and smear it over the base with kitchen paper.

Squeeze the outline of a heart into the pan, then add dots around the edges. Pipe swirls, crosses or whatever pattern you like inside the heart.

When the batter has set and is golden underneath, flip it over with a palette knife. Continue to cook the other side for a minute or so until completely cooked. Slide on to a plate and keep warm while you make the other pancakes, re-oiling the pan and refilling the squeezy bottle as necessary.

Serve dusted with icing sugar.

Cook's tip
If you don't have a squeezy bottle, make a round pancake instead. To shape it into a heart, fold it into quarters, then carve a rounded 'v' into the top.

HEART PALMIERS

These light pastry treats, also known as palm trees and elephant ears, can easily be formed into heart shapes with a pinch of the pastry.

MAKES ABOUT 20

320g ready-rolled puff pastry
60g almond or peanut butter
50g dark chocolate (about 50% cocoa solids),
  chopped
1 heaped tbsp golden caster sugar
15g whole almonds, finely chopped
zest of 1 orange
demerara sugar, for sprinkling
a little flour for dusting

Line 2 baking sheets with baking parchment.

Lightly flour a clean work surface and unroll the puff pastry on it. Spread the almond or peanut butter all over the pastry using a palette knife and leaving a 1cm border around each side. Sprinkle over the dark chocolate, sugar, chopped almonds and orange zest, pressing these bits into the nut butter with the back of a spoon.

Roll the long sides of the pastry inwards to the middle of the sheet, leaving a 5mm gap between the 2 rolls. Transfer the rolled pastry on to a prepared baking sheet and chill in the fridge for 20 minutes.

Preheat the oven to 220°C/200°C fan/gas 7.

HEART PALMIERS CONTINUED

Once the pastry has chilled, transfer it to
a board and trim the ends so that they're
even. Starting at one end, carefully cut into
1cm-thick slices. Lay each slice flat on the
second baking sheet, squeezing the pastry to
a point at the bottom and pressing the rolled
parts together to create a long heart shape.
At this stage I think the rolls look a little bit
like the head in Edvard Munch's 'Scream', but
don't worry: they puff up and become heart-
shaped as they bake.

Sprinkle the hearts with demerara sugar,
then bake for about 20 minutes, until golden
and crisp. Cool on a wire rack and store in an
airtight container for up to 3 days.

BLACKBERRY HEARTS IN CREAM JELLIES

Home-made jellies are a treat, and these ones, made from a fresh fruit purée and evaporated milk, mean you can use whatever fruit you fancy. Serve with a scoop of vanilla ice cream.

SERVES 4

6 gelatine leaves
150g blackberries
2 tbsp golden caster sugar
225ml evaporated milk
vanilla ice cream, to serve

You will need
muffin tin
4 small paper cases
plastic tray, about the size of a margarine tub
4cm heart-shaped cutter

Soak 2 of the gelatine leaves in a bowl of cold water, and do the same with another 2 leaves in a separate bowl. Set aside for 10 minutes.

Purée the blackberries in a blender and strain through a sieve to remove the seeds. Stir in half the sugar, then weigh the purée and make up to 100g with water.

Put the blackberry mixture in a small pan over a medium heat and bring to a simmer. As soon as it is hot (just a minute or so), take off the heat. Lift the gelatine out of one of the bowls of water, squeeze out the excess liquid and stir the gelatine into the blackberry mixture until it dissolves. Set aside to cool.

Pour half the evaporated milk into a pan and bring to the boil. Turn off the heat and stir in half the remaining sugar. Squeeze out the remaining soaked gelatine and stir into the milk mixture until dissolved. Set aside to cool.

BLACKBERRY HEARTS CONTINUED

Place 4 paper cases in a muffin tin. Divide the evaporated milk mixture evenly among them and set aside.

Pour the cooled blackberry purée into a small plastic tray or empty margarine tub. It needs to be big enough to cut 4 hearts out of it using a 4cm cutter later. Chill in the fridge for 2–3 hours until set.

When the blackberry jelly has set, stamp out 4 hearts with a 4cm cutter and place each one on top of an evaporated milk jelly.

Soak the last 2 gelatine leaves in a bowl of cold water for 10 minutes. Heat the remaining evaporated milk in a pan over a medium heat and stir in the remaining sugar. Lift the gelatine out of the bowl and squeeze out the excess water, then stir the gelatine into the milk mixture until dissolved. Set aside to cool.

Carefully pour the cooled liquid around the hearts and return to the fridge to set.

Serve with a ball of vanilla ice cream.

SOPAPILLAS

These little fried breads are South America's answer to doughnuts. Serve with a refreshing berry coulis to dip them into.

MAKES ABOUT 20

150g plain flour, plus extra for dusting
1 tsp baking powder
a good pinch of salt
1 tbsp white vegetable fat
about 100ml water
vegetable oil for deep frying
caster sugar for dusting

For the berry coulis
200g frozen summer fruits, thawed
1 tbsp cassis
1 tbsp icing sugar

You will need
4cm heart-shaped cutter

Sift the flour, baking powder and salt into a large bowl. Rub the vegetable fat into the mixture until it resembles breadcrumbs. Stir in enough water to make a soft, sticky dough, then knead on a lightly floured board until smooth. Shape into a ball, place in a clean bowl, cover and leave to rest at room temperature for at least 1 hour.

To make the coulis, put the summer fruits, cassis and icing sugar in a blender and whiz together. Strain through a sieve into a bowl.

Divide the rested dough into 4 equal pieces. Roll out each piece on a lightly floured work surface until about 2mm thick, then stamp out hearts using a 4cm cutter.

Heat a one-third depth of vegetable oil to 190°C in a pan or deep-fat fryer (or until a cube of bread dropped into the oil sizzles and turns golden within 10 seconds). Slide 3–4 hearts into the hot oil and cook for about 1 minute, until golden. Lift out with a slotted spoon and drain on kitchen paper. Cook all the remaining hearts in the same way.

Serve in a small pile, dusted with caster sugar, with the raspberry coulis on the side.

LOVELY LUNCHBOX MUFFINS

Shaping a muffin into a heart is easy with a clever manoeuvre of the baking case and a piece of scrunched-up foil. Serve with heart-shaped sandwiches filled with ham, cheese and cucumber.

MAKES 12 MUFFINS

125g light soft brown sugar
2 eggs
100ml olive oil
200g plain flour
1 tsp baking powder
1 tsp cinnamon
½ tsp ground mixed spice
a good grating of nutmeg
150g carrots, grated
75g sultanas
zest of 1 orange

You will need
12-hole muffin tin
12 small paper cases

Preheat the oven to 180°C/160°C fan/gas 4. Line a 12-hole muffin tin with paper cases. Roll up 12 small pieces of foil and shape them into triangular wedges the same depth as the cases (see overleaf).

Put the sugar, eggs and olive oil in a large bowl and beat well until combined. Sift in the flour, baking powder and spices, then stir in the carrots, sultanas and orange zest. Spoon the mixture evenly into the muffin cases.

To make the heart shapes, push a wedge of foil into the side of each case to create a 'v' shape.

Bake in the oven for about 30 minutes, until golden and a skewer inserted into the centre comes out clean. Transfer the muffins in their cases to a wire rack to cool. Sprinkle with a little extra cinnamon before serving.

SAVOURY

LOVEHEART SALT AND PEPPER BAGELS WITH ROASTED TOMATO SOUP

The roasting method for this soup works a treat, leaving the vegetables caramelised, sweet and full of flavour.

SERVES 4

1 tsp dried yeast
2 tbsp golden caster sugar
175ml warm water
250g strong white or wholemeal bread flour,
   plus extra for dusting
½ tsp salt, plus extra for sprinkling
½ tsp freshly ground black pepper, plus extra
   for sprinkling
1 tsp sesame seeds
1 tbsp vegetable oil

For the soup
2 tbsp olive oil
1 large onion, roughly chopped
4 large tomatoes
1 red pepper
2 whole garlic cloves
200ml tomato passata
600ml hot vegetable stock
a couple of dashes of Tabasco sauce
salt and freshly ground black pepper

To make the bagels, put the yeast in a small bowl with 1 tsp of the sugar and 100ml of the warm water. Set aside for 10 minutes to allow the yeast to activate.

Sift the flour into a large bowl and stir in the salt, pepper and sesame seeds. Make a well in the middle and pour in the yeast mixture, along with the remaining warm water. Mix well with a spoon or round-bladed knife to make a rough dough, then knead well on a lightly floured surface until smooth. Cover and set aside to rise for 1 hour.

Oil a non-stick baking sheet. Punch down the risen dough and divide into 12 equal pieces. Roll each one into a 25cm 'sausage' then curl the ends together to form a heart shape. Place on the oiled baking sheet and allow to rise for 15 minutes.

Preheat the grill until medium hot. Grill the top of the bagels for 2–3 minutes.

Preheat the oven to 190°C/170°C fan/gas 5.

LOVEHEART SALT AND PEPPER BAGELS
CONTINUED

Bring a large pan of water to the boil and
stir in the remaining sugar. Carefully lower
the bagels into the water in batches and cook
for 1–2 minutes. Lift out, drain well and place
back on the oiled baking sheet. Sprinkle
the bagels with a little coarsely ground salt
and pepper. Bake in the oven for about
15 minutes, until golden and the bases sound
hollow when tapped. Transfer to a wire rack
to cool.

To make the soup, preheat the oven to
200°C/180°C fan/gas 6.

Put the oil in a large roasting tin and add
the onion, tomatoes, red pepper and garlic
cloves. Season well and toss the vegetables in
the oil. Roast in the oven for 30 minutes, or
until tender. Stir in the stock and passata and
continue to cook for a further 10 minutes.

Set the tin aside to cool for 5 minutes, then
whiz the contents in a blender until smooth,
adding more stock if necessary. Pour the
soup into a pan and heat gently, adding the
Tabasco and more seasoning to taste. Serve
with the warm bagels.

SUMMER LOVE MINESTRONE WITH PESTO

This is a delicious, rustic, tomato-based soup made with chunky borlotti beans and alphabet pasta. You can spell out any message you like. Serve with crusty bread.

SERVES 4

1 onion, diced
1 celery stick, diced
1 carrot, diced
1 garlic clove, crushed
a sprig of rosemary
a sprig of thyme
400g tin chopped tomatoes
1 tbsp tomato purée
400ml hot vegetable stock
50ml dry white wine
400g tin borlotti beans, drained
125g alphabet pasta
4 runner beans, finely sliced
olive oil for frying
salt and freshly ground black pepper

For the pesto
15g basil leaves
100ml olive oil
25g Parmesan
25g pine nuts

Heat some olive oil in a big frying pan and fry the onion, celery and carrot over a medium heat for 5–10 minutes, until they start to caramelise. Stir in the crushed garlic, rosemary and thyme and season well. Stir in the chopped tomatoes, tomato purée, vegetable stock, white wine and borlotti beans. Cover and bring to the boil. Simmer for 15 minutes. Stir in the alphabet pasta and runner beans and simmer for 3–4 minutes, or until the pasta is cooked. Season to taste.

Make the pesto by whizzing the basil, olive oil, Parmesan and pine nuts together in a blender. Season to taste.

Ladle the minestrone into 4 bowls. Pull a little bit of tomato to the surface and use it as a raft fro the pasta letters of whatever message you want to spell out. Spoon a heart-shaped mound of pesto on top and serve.

RICOTTA AND HERB RAVIOLI

Fresh pasta takes minutes to knock up. Just remember to roll it thinly because it swells when cooked. These ravioli are ready when they bob to the surface of the water.

SERVES 2

100g '00' flour, plus extra for dusting
1 egg
½ tsp olive oil
75g ricotta cheese
15g pecorino cheese, freshly grated
2 tbsp chopped herbs, such as parsley, thyme and chives, plus extra to garnish
salt and freshly ground black pepper

For the dressing
1–2 tbsp extra-virgin olive oil
2 tomatoes, seeded and chopped
1 tbsp pine nuts, toasted
a squeeze of lemon juice

You will need
7cm heart-shaped cutter

Lightly dust a board with flour. Put the pasta flour into a bowl or food processor and add the egg and olive oil. Beat or whiz together until the mixture resembles breadcrumbs. Use your hands to bring the mixture together, then knead on a floured surface until the dough feels stiff. Wrap in cling film and set aside to rest for 20 minutes.

Beat together the ricotta, pecorino, herbs and seasoning in a bowl.

Cut the dough into 8 equal pieces and roll them out to a thickness of 2mm. Carefully stamp out large hearts using a 7cm cutter or sharp knife, rerolling the pasta as necessary.

Spoon a little of the ricotta mixture into the centre of one of the hearts. Brush around the edges with a little water, then lay a second heart loosely over the top. Working quickly, press it around the mound of filling to push out any air and seal the edges. Repeat until all the ravioli are filled, then transfer to a wire rack and set aside to dry for 30 minutes.

RICOTTA AND HERB RAVIOLI CONTINUED

Bring a large pan of salted water to the boil. Gently lower the ravioli into the pan and cook for 3–5 minutes. They're ready when they've all floated to the surface.

Meanwhile, make the dressing. Heat the oil in a frying pan. Add the tomatoes and pine nuts and cook for 1–2 minutes. Season well and stir in the lemon juice.

Lift the ravioli out of the pan, drain well and divide between 2 plates. Spoon over the tomato dressing, sprinkle over a few more chopped herbs and serve immediately.

ROSE-LOVER'S SALAD WITH BOILED EGG HEARTS

Shaping an egg into a heart is easy with this clever technique, using a wooden skewer, a piece of card and a couple of elastic bands.

SERVES 2

2 large eggs
2 tomatoes
a handful of radishes
a small chunk of cucumber
½ red pepper, seeded
4–6 slices of salami
a small handful of green beans, trimmed
a handful of watercress

For the dressing
1½ tbsp extra-virgin olive oil
1 tsp wholegrain mustard
1 tsp white wine vinegar
1 tsp cold water
salt and freshly ground black pepper

You will need
stiff card
2 skewers
4 elastic bands

About an hour before you want to serve the salad, boil the eggs in boiling water for 7 minutes, until hard. Cool quickly in a bowl of cold water, then peel.

Cut out 2 pieces of card about 14 x 10cm and fold each piece in half lengthways. Open out the card and position a cooked egg lengthways along the fold. Balance a skewer lengthways on the egg and press it down (not too hard) to create an indent. Bring up the sides of the card and secure the skewer with an elastic band at either end. Chill for at least 15 minutes.

Using a small sharp knife, peel the skin from the tomatoes in long, thin strips, then roll the strips up to make rose shapes.

Carve tiny hearts from the radishes, cucumber and red pepper. Cut each slice of salami into quarters. Cut rounded 'v' shapes in the top of each quarter to create hearts.

Simmer the beans in boiling water until tender.

Drain and roughly chop.

Take the eggs from the fridge, remove the cards and skewers and slice the eggs widthways into heart shapes.

Arrange the hearts, roses and green beans on 2 plates, then drape watercress around the ingredients to fill in the gaps.

Whisk together the dressing ingredients. Season well and drizzle over the salad. Enjoy!

HIS AND HERS BREKKIE

A wonderfully easy and
eye-catching eggy breakfast.

SERVES 2

4 slices of white or brown bread
1 egg
1–2 tbsp milk
vegetable oil
a knob of butter

For the fried egg
1 slice of bread
1 egg
vegetable oil

To serve
a few slices of peach
a little icing sugar
1 tomato, halved and grilled

You will need
6cm cutter
7cm cutter

Use a 6cm cutter to stamp out 3–4 hearts from the 4 slices of bread (whiz the offcuts to make breadcrumbs and freeze to use another time). Beat the egg and milk together in a bowl and dip the hearts into the mixture.

Heat a little oil and butter in a frying pan. Once the butter has melted, swirl it around the pan to cover the base. Fry the hearts in batches until golden on each side, then set aside on a warm plate.

For the fried egg, cut a heart shape out of the middle of a slice of bread using a 7cm cutter and set the heart aside. Toast the bread lightly on both sides, then heat a little oil in the frying pan. Break the egg into a cup. Put the toast in the pan and slide the egg into the heart cut-out, taking care not to overfill it. Cover and cook for a couple of minutes, until the white is set.

To serve, arrange the French toast on a plate with some peach slices and a dusting of icing sugar. Place the fried egg toast on another plate with the grilled tomato halves.

LUXURY FISH PIE

These delicious pies are made with soft fillets of plaice bathed in a creamy cheese sauce and topped with smooth mashed potato.

SERVES 2

3 medium potatoes (about 300g), chopped
30g butter
200ml milk, plus extra for the mash
15g flour
25g Parmesan
50ml double cream
a large handful of spinach
300g plaice fillets, skinned
salt and freshly ground black pepper

You will need
300ml heart-shaped pie dishes
  or 600ml pie dish

Put the potatoes in a pan of cold water, cover and bring to the boil. Simmer until tender (about 15 minutes), then drain and stir in 10g of the butter and a splash of milk. Season well and mash until smooth.

Melt the remaining butter in a pan over a low heat and stir in the flour. Cook for 1 minute, then take the pan off the heat and slowly stir in the rest of the milk. Return the pan to the heat and bring to the boil, stirring constantly. Simmer for a few minutes, until thickened, then stir in the Parmesan, cream and spinach. Take the pan off the heat.

Preheat the oven to 190°C/170°C fan/gas 5. Season the fish fillets, then roll them up and place in the pie dishes. Cover with the sauce, spoon the mash over the top and shape the surface into a pattern of fish scales using the tip of a knife.

Bake for about 20 minutes, until golden and the pie is hot all the way through.

BRAVEHEART PIE

The rich beef stew in this pie is sweetened with cranberries and seasoned with rosemary. The lid is made with overlapping hearts of pastry.

SERVES 4–6

1–2 tbsp olive oil
1 onion, chopped
1 celery stick, chopped
1 heaped tbsp plain flour, plus extra for dusting
700g braising beef, cubed
100ml white wine
500ml hot beef stock
1 tsp tomato purée
a dash of Worcestershire sauce
25g dried cranberries
a sprig of rosemary
300g ready-made shortcrust pastry
1 egg, beaten
salt and freshly ground black pepper

You will need
23cm pie dish
4cm heart-shaped cutter
pie funnel (optional)

Heat 1 tbsp of the olive oil in a flameproof casserole dish and stir fry the onion and celery for 5 minutes over a medium heat. Season well and spoon into a bowl.

Spoon the flour into a clean bowl, season well, then toss the beef in it. Heat another drizzle of oil in the pan and brown the beef in batches until dark brown on all sides. Don't stint at this stage as the browning is essential to give the stew a rich, deep flavour. Set each batch aside until all the pieces are done.

Add the wine to the empty pan. Bring to a simmer and scrape up all the crusty bits on the bottom. Return the beef, onion and celery mixture to the pan, and stir in the stock, tomato purée and Worcestershire sauce. Add the cranberries and rosemary, cover, bring to the boil, then cover and simmer very gently for 1½–2 hours.

If you have a pie funnel, place it in the middle of a 23cm pie dish. Using a slotted spoon, transfer the meat to the dish. Simmer the sauce in the pan for about 5 minutes, until it has reduced by a third, then pour it over the meat.

Preheat the oven to 220°C/200°C fan/gas 7.

Lightly flour a work surface. Cut off a small piece of pastry dough and roll it out until it's a couple of millimetres thick. Slice it into strips the same width as the rim of the pie dish. Brush around the edge of the dish with the beaten egg and stick the pastry strips around it to create a frame for your pie. Roll out the remaining dough to a thickness of 3mm and cut out hearts using a 4cm cutter, and rerolling as necessary.

Brush the pastry border with more beaten egg, then arrange the hearts in concentric circles, working from the edge towards the middle. You might find it useful to put a couple of small pastry strips around the funnel, on top of the meat, before positioning the last few hearts.

Brush the top of the pie with beaten egg, then bake for about 30 minutes, until the hearts are golden all over.

Cook's tip
If you have a pressure cooker and would like to save some time, cook the beef mixture in it for 40–45 minutes, or according to the manufacturer's instructions.

FISH-LOVER'S PASTA

Choose whichever fish you fancy for this simple and flavoursome dish – just remember to keep a couple of prawns whole to create a heart shape at the end.

SERVES 2

2 handfuls of raw prawns
2 tsp olive oil
1 garlic clove, sliced
250g tomato passata
100ml hot fish or chicken stock
a generous glug of dry white wine
125g angel hair pasta
125g white fish, such as haddock, cut into
   bite-sized chunks
a handful of clams, washed
1–2 tbsp freshly chopped dill
salmon eggs
salt and freshly ground black pepper
extra-virgin olive oil for drizzling

Set aside 2 whole prawns in their shells, then peel the remainder and set aside.

Bring a large pan of salted water to the boil.

Heat the olive oil in a pan and cook the garlic for 1 minute. Stir in the passata, hot stock and white wine. Season well and bring to the boil.

Add the pasta to the pan of boiling water and cook according to packet instructions.

Stir the fish, clams and all the prawns into the tomato mixture and cover with a lid. Cook over a low heat until all the clams have opened and the prawns have turned from grey to pink (about 5 minutes).

FISH-LOVER'S PASTA CONTINUED

Drain the cooked pasta well, return it to the
pan and stir in a little extra-virgin olive oil and
some salt. Spoon most of the fish and sauce
into the pasta. Take a large spoon and fork and
twirl spoonfuls of the pasta on to a large platter,
tweaking the swirls to create a heart shape.

Spoon over the remaining sauce and position
the whole prawns in the middle of the pasta in
a heart shape. Garnish with the dill, dot with
the salmon eggs and drizzle of extra-virgin
olive oil.

HEARTBURGER IN A BUN

This is a fun way of serving
a classic American diner dish.
Ketchup's a must!

SERVES 2

250g beef mince
1 shallot, finely chopped
½ tsp Italian mixed herbs
2 burger buns or seeded rolls
mayonnaise
slices of lettuce
a few slices of red onion
2 cherry tomatoes, halved
2 gherkins, sliced
oil, for frying

For the chips
2 potatoes, cut into finger length pieces
a little oil, plus extra to cook the burger
vegetable oil
salt and freshly ground black pepper

First make the chips. Preheat the oven to 200°C/180°C fan/gas 6. Line a shallow roasting tin with baking parchment.

Toss the potatoes in a little oil and season well. Spread out in the roasting tin and roast for 20–30 minutes, until golden, turning them halfway through.

Break the mince up in a bowl and stir in the chopped shallot, mixed herbs and a little salt and pepper. Divide the mixture in half and shape into hearts, making sure they are not more than 2cm thick.

Drizzle a little oil into a frying pan over a medium heat and fry the burgers for 3–4 minutes on each side until cooked to your liking.

Slice the buns in half and spread the lower halves with a little mayonnaise. Add some lettuce, red onion and tomato, then top with the burger, some gherkin slices and the remaining bun halves on the side. Serve with the chips.

BIG HEART PIZZA WITH TRUFFLE

For a really crisp base, heat the oven to its highest temperature and cook the pizzas on a preheated baking sheet to mimic the effect of a wood-fired oven. The final addition of truffle adds a wonderfully luxurious flavour.

SERVES 2

¾ tsp dried yeast
a pinch of sugar
135ml warm water
200g strong bread flour, plus extra for dusting
½ tsp salt
1 tsp olive oil

For the topping
4–6 tbsp tomato passata
½ garlic clove, crushed
2 large handfuls of baby leaf spinach
1 ball of mozzarella, sliced
2 eggs
truffle shavings or truffle oil
extra-virgin olive oil
salt and freshly ground black pepper

Put the yeast in a bowl with the sugar. Pour in the warm water and stir. Set aside for 10 minutes to allow the yeast to activate. It will thicken and look frothy when ready.

Sift the flour into a large clean bowl and stir in the salt. Make a well in the centre and pour in the olive oil along with the yeast mixture. Stir with a table knife to make a craggy dough, then bring together with your hands, mopping up any bits. Transfer the dough to a board and knead until it's smooth and elastic. You shouldn't need any extra flour at this stage, but if it's really sticky, dust with a little more. Place the dough in a clean bowl, cover and set aside for 15 minutes.

Preheat the oven to its highest setting and heat 2 baking sheets.

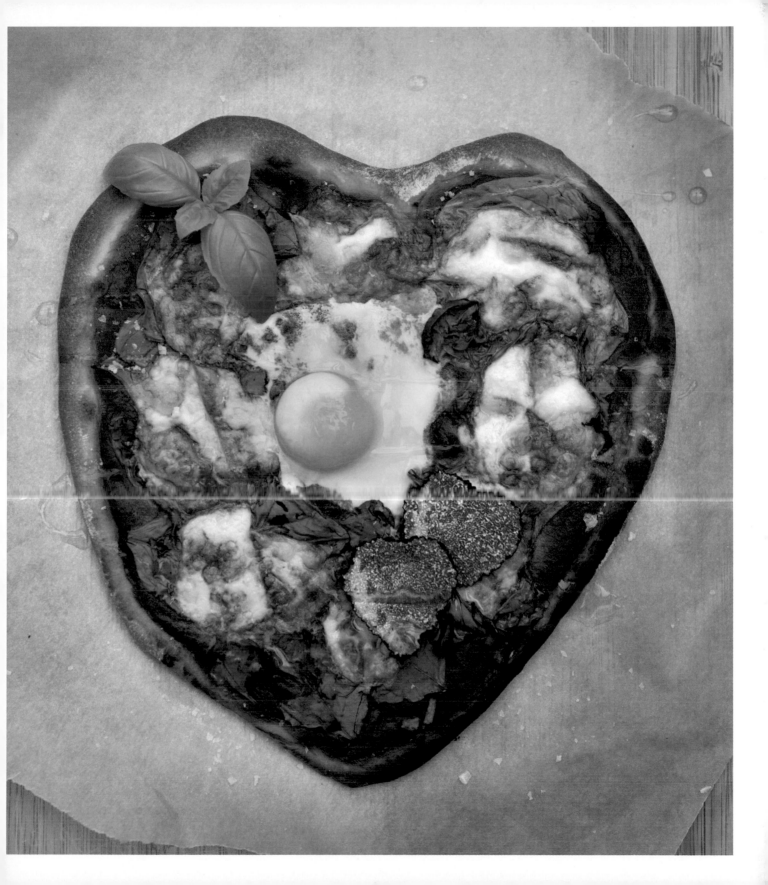

BIG HEART PIZZA WITH TRUFFLE CONTINUED

Divide the dough in half and roll each piece into a rough circle on a lightly floured sheet of baking parchment. Take the middle of one side and tuck it down slightly towards the centre to create a heart shape. Do the same with the other circle.

To make the topping, mix the passata and crushed garlic together and season well. Spread evenly over the pizza bases, smoothing it with the back of the spoon. Place half the spinach around the edge of each pizza, then top with the mozzarella. Slide the pieces of baking parchment on to the preheated baking sheets. Bake for 10 minutes, then remove from the oven and crack an egg into the middle of each pizza. Return to the oven for another 3–5 minutes, until the egg is cooked to your liking.

To serve, drizzle over the extra virgin olive oil and garnish with shavings of truffle or a drizzle of truffle oil.

FIVE-SPICE DUCK HEART PIE POPS

These mini pies are baked on sticks. Chicken, beef or pork would all work well if you don't have duck.

MAKES 8

1 duck breast
1 tsp ground white pepper
1 tsp sea salt
1 garlic clove, crushed
1cm piece fresh root ginger, grated
¼ tsp Chinese five-spice powder
2–3 tbsp hoisin sauce, plus extra for dipping
1 tsp sesame oil
1 tsp rice wine vinegar
200g ready-made shortcrust pastry
1 egg, beaten
vegetable oil for drizzling
plain flour for dusting
black and white sesame seeds for sprinkling

You will need
5cm heart-shaped cutter
6cm heart-shaped cutter
8 wooden skewers

Preheat the oven to 200°C/180°C fan/gas 6 and place a baking sheet in the oven.

Prick the duck all over with a fork, then rub the pepper, salt, garlic, ginger and five-spice into the skin. Place in a roasting tin, drizzle with vegetable oil and roast for 40 minutes. Set aside to cool.

Shred 75g of meat from the breast (you can freeze any leftovers). Place the shredded duck in a bowl and stir in the hoisin sauce, sesame oil and vinegar.

Lightly dust a board with flour and roll out the pastry until it's about 2cm thick. Cut out 8 hearts using a 5cm cutter, and 8 hearts using a 6cm cutter, rerolling as necessary.

Divide the duck between the 5cm pastry hearts. Press a skewer into the base of each one, then brush a little beaten egg around the edges. Top each one with a 6cm heart, pressing down lightly and crimping the edges. Brush the hearts with beaten egg and sprinkle over the seeds.

Place on the preheated baking sheet and bake for about 20 minutes, until golden. Cool a little then serve with extra hoisin sauce for dipping.

STEAK FRITES POUR DEUX

Add some romance to a steak dinner with golden, heart-shaped 'chips'.

SERVES 2

150g rump or fillet steaks
2 medium potatoes
a few sprigs of thyme
2 shallots, finely sliced
a knob of butter
75ml red wine
1 tsp redcurrant jelly
olive oil for drizzling
salt and freshly ground black pepper
salad leaves or vegetables of your choice, to
    serve

For the mustard mayo
250ml olive oil
2 egg yolks, beaten
1 tsp wholegrain mustard
1 tbsp lemon juice

You will need
2.5–3cm heart-shaped cutter

Preheat the oven to 200°C/180°C fan/gas 6. Take the steak out of the fridge to come up to room temperature. Line a roasting tin with baking parchment.

Slice the potatoes lengthways about 4mm thick. Use a 2.5–3cm cutter to stamp out hearts (keep the offcuts for a soup or roast on a separate tray) and place them in the roasting tin. Drizzle with olive oil and toss to coat. Season well and scatter over the thyme. Roast for about 20 minutes, until golden, turning them halfway through.

To make the mayonnaise, add a drop of the oil to the egg yolks and beat together. Continue to add the oil, drop by drop beating constantly. Once the mixture emulsifies and thickens, start to add the oil in a steady drizzle. When all the oil has been incorporated and the mayonnaise is thick, stir in the mustard and lemon juice and season to taste.

STEAK FRITES POUR DEUX CONTINUED

Heat a frying pan until hot, then add a drizzle
of olive oil and swirl it around. Add the sliced
shallots and stir-fry until crisp and golden.
Tip on to a plate and set aside.

Add the steaks to the pan and fry for
3–5 minutes on each side, depending on
thickness and how well done you like them.
Transfer to a warm plate to rest.

Add the butter, red wine and redcurrant jelly
to the pan, scraping up all the bits in the
bottom with a wooden spoon, and simmer
until syrupy. Add any juices from the rested
steak and stir again

Place a steak on each serving plate, spoon
over the shallots and sauce and serve with
the potatoes, mayo and some salad leaves
or vegetables on the side.

CHAMPAGNE-LOVER'S TREAT

These little baked nibbles are originally from Puglia in Italy, where they're known as *tarali*. They are usually circular, but here, of course, they are heart-shaped. Serve with bowls of spiced nuts and olives and glasses of chilled champagne.

SERVES 2, WITH PLENTY OF LEFTOVERS

100g plain flour, plus extra for dusting
½ tsp salt
2 tbsp dry white wine
2 tbsp olive oil
chilled champagne, to serve

For the olives
100g olives
1 tbsp extra-virgin olive oil
a sprig of rosemary, roughly chopped
¼ lemon, thinly sliced
½ tsp fennel seeds
a good pinch of salt

For the spiced nuts
100g mixed nuts
½ tsp smoked paprika
a pinch of chilli flakes
olive oil
salt and freshly ground black pepper

First make the olives. Mix together all the ingredients for them in a sealable container, then chill.

Sift the flour for the tarali into a bowl and stir in the salt. Make a well in the middle and pour in the white wine and olive oil. Stir thoroughly, then knead the mixture to make a smooth dough. Place in a bowl, cover and set aside for 1 hour.

Meanwhile, make the spiced nuts. Preheat the oven to 200°C/180°C fan/gas 6. Line a baking sheet with baking parchment.

Put the nuts in a large roasting tin with the paprika, chilli flakes and a drizzle of olive oil. Season well and toss all the ingredients together. Roast in the oven for 10–15 minutes, until the nuts are golden, shaking the pan halfway through. Set aside to cool.

Break off walnut-sized pieces of the rested dough and roll each piece into a 15cm 'sausage'. Join the ends of each sausage to form the curved parts of a heart, then pinch the bottom to create the point. Place the tarali on the prepared baking sheet and bake for 15 minutes, until golden.

Place the olives, nuts and biscuits in separate bowls, pop the champagne, pour and serve.

ZESTY ICE HEARTS

This recipe makes 2 different flavours of ice cubes – orange citrus, and lime and lemon. They melt quickly, so pop a couple of regular ice cubes in with them to help keep the drink chilled.

SERVES 2

zest and juice of 2 oranges
zest and juice of 3 lemons
zest and juice of 3 limes

To serve
a long drinks such as tonic water, lemonade
  or gin and tonic
lemon or lime slices

You will need
heart-shaped ice-cube tray

Pour the orange juice and zest into a small jug. Add 1 tbsp each of lemon and lime juice and a good pinch of lemon and lime zest. Pour into half the ice-cube holes.

Mix together the remaining lemon and lime zest and juice and fill the other holes.

Freeze the tray overnight.

Serve in a long glass with a drink of your choice and slices of lemon or lime.

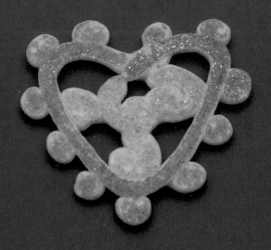

Special thanks to Suzannah, Dan, Pearl and
Wilfred Rich; Kevan Westbury; Caroline for the
lovely commission; Trish Burgess for the edit;
Sarah for the photos; Anna for the design and
Ellie for her invaluable help in the kitchen.